STRAY THOUGHTS

Poetic epiphanies.

Udayachandran C.P.

A few words:

If my memory serves me right, I did not approach anyone with a petition to create me, or bring me into this world!

This world created me of its own will.

Naturally, the world cannot disown me after its decision to give life to me. I can and do claim my right over the world, as anyone else can and does.

Having arrived, I do cling to my right to have a space of my own in this world, however trifling and finite it is. And within that space given to me, like a spider, I create an exclusive world of mine. And that becomes the world of mine, displacing the explicit one at large.

Long or short, everyone in the world weaves a web of yarns. Willingly or unwillingly! Knowingly or unknowingly! Creating yarns that outlive time is exclusive to the human race.

Some choose to hold on to them and keep them close to their chests. Some tend to talk aloud about them. I just happen to belong to the latter category.

And here are my tales. Mostly in free verse form. Maybe they are not as colourful or perceptive as the ones created in my era or earlier. But to me, they are special. Because, they are my offsprings, my creations, my dreams, and here I spread them out before you. I am incapable of saying anything more than what these borrowed words of the supreme poet, Yeats, can convey: "Tread softly, because you tread on my dreams."

I dedicate this small effort as an act of consolation to my late parents who expected me to do a lot more things that I was never ever capable of.

My apologies to them, and to the WORLD!

<u>1. A flash of love, so sudden…</u>

Like a flash of lightning from the blues,
You struck me flat.
I winced not,
As true as earth, I was silent,
Quiet, and patient.

Branching into a thousand serpents,
In a flash, you moved in,
Coiling around me, like a Boa Constrictor.
So wild the clutch was,
It left me numb and breathless.

Yet I chose not to battle,
For I found a charm in suffocation,
Hard of resistance.
The venom you had injected into me by then
Mixed with the blood
and dulled me into a daze.

Perhaps the stupor; Perhaps not.
Why? Does it matter?

What the flash at a distance,
unwinding from the heights,
Wrote so brilliant in
a thousand hues was this.
What the rumbling growl
Told me so sharp and clear was this
"In love you surrender. So you conquer!
In love you lose. So you win!
<u>In love you die. So you live!"</u>

2. Dementia.

Dementia
is an attitude of mind.
It is a change of state
from normality to super-normality.

Breaking mental morbidity,
to give life to the wildest dreams,
Let us say farewellto the too sound world,
and drown in the ocean of silence!

In that unsound world,
let us compress ourselves to become
that tiny primordial speck of dust,
oblivious of the sense of space and time!

Listen!
There is just this murmur,
the murmur of impatience, of self melting into self.
Listen!
There is just this murmur,
the murmur of impatience.
the bumbling of a bubble,
caught in the reverie of a Big Bang!
To expand...
To conquer...,
The realms of fantasy.

Come, let us add
dementia to our dimension.
And have a black hole of imagination!

3. Do not open that closet!

Do Not Open That Closet!

Do not open that closet of
Dreams, Hopes and Sighs!

Do not open that closet
In which are safely shackled
Benumbed dreams
Of the Past and the Living!

Do not open that Closet
In which are firmly fettered
Hopes of humanity
Crushed and mauled!

Do not open that closet
Within which is deeply buried
Aggrieved sighs of
The Massacred and the Oppressed!

Do not open that closet
And free them.

They will wreak havoc
On our INNOCENT WORLD!

4. When the world finds you amoral...

There were times I thought I was balanced.
Fine, let me rescript it.
Kind of balanced.

There were times I thought I was fair.
Agreed, let me confess.
Somewhat fair.

There were times I thought I was upright.
Okay, let me correct.
Fairly upright.

But those were times!
I am convinced it's no more the same.
Evident and for certain.

The world now tells me that I am vicious.
And I stand convinced that I am bad.
Out and out poison.
That I am incorrigible,
A menace to the world.

What else can I gauge when
My family, friends and other pals
Flood me with thoughts and advices,
With no mission other than
To change the beast in me.

They have but just a lofty thought.
To refine me. To mend me. To transform me.
For, They are the souls UPRIGHT.
For, They are the quintessence of BALANCE.
For, They are the paragons of VIRTUE.

It is their birth-right. It is their life-mission.
To refine me, the Poison.
To mend me, the Incorrigible.

It's like a war.
No, it is war.
Me, the fiend, on one side.
Them, the genteel angels, on the other.
They have declared an electronic war on me.
An assault, a non-stop one.

They keep shooting thoughts so sublime through
Whatsapp,
Every now and then.
They cover the ground,
carpet bombing me with edifying tweets,
Almost like a train.

They charge, Unleashing a jet of mails
Carrying ideas, inspiring,
Like a convocation of eagles landing on its prey.

Because that is their mission.
To deliver me.

What if they do not get time to grasp the messages
themselves?
What if they cannot translate
The stirring thoughts into action themselves?
What if they cannot transform themselves?

In times of war, is not the enemy alone the focus?
<u>In times of war, is not winning the war, the supreme?</u>

5. God loves drunks.

No wonder, God loves drunks.
Drunks are epitomes of innocence.

They are just undeniably guileless.
And so much artlessly plain.

For a drunk,
Left or right, he will be right every time,
And, right or left, he can never be left behind.

Yes, the drunk is starry-eyed.
Looking up at the blue and the stars,
He just takes a deep breath,
And he has his head too, full of stars.

But, a drunk is not ever dazzled
By the sky and stars.

His choice is loud and clear.
He is humble to embrace the poor earth.

He hugs it, takes it lying down,
and kisses it a hundred times,
saying, "I know, I know,
This is just a trial and mock-drill,
My final abode is there with you!"

6. Relationships.

Relationships are like draughts of wind.

Some are gentle wafts.
They approach you so mildly,
Touching you so feathery.
You wonder where it came from,
Whither it went.
You are sadder now that it came,
staying so short,
And leaving without a trace.

Some of them, you can see coming.
There is a beginning and an end.
The drama builds up. The air thickens.
The wind comes with a howl and rocks you.
It churns and breaks you, as it lashes.
The air then clears gradually,
Rays of light peeping though
gaps between dark clouds.
You heave a sigh of relief
As the rumbles move away and away.

Some are tender whiffs.
They approach you so mellow,
with a caress and a pat so fuzzy.
A gentle hug that never releases.
You never know if the waft left you.
<u>The fragrance lingers ever after!</u>

7. Silent speak.

The essence of life, they assert,
is in its clamour and din.
Roars and bellows are what provide
life its real meaning and purpose.

For them,
silence is a disturbing sensation.
And an ear-shattering drum.

Tender-hearted as they are,
they are chasing you, baying after you,
Charging at you, yelling and shouting.
with the sole intent of
cloaking your eerie, disturbing silence!

It's to render meaning to
your quiet and hushed life,
that they swoop down on you in droves,
To pull out that muzzled breath
out of your windpipe
and give it a vibrant high pitch note.

If they are successful in converting it to
a never-ending shrill shriek
that penetrates the world,
a resonating squeal that floats in the air,
they would consider it eminently fulfilling
to have made you
and your otherwise futile life
speakingly expressive!

<u>8. The entry and exit.</u>

Yes, people do come.
Silently.
And so they go.
Silently.
And a lot of them,
with barely any trace.

But there are some who
make a statement of their life.
Some drawing a colourful painting of it!
Some play a soulful tune with their lives.
While some make a roll of it
with sound and fury.
A lot of it!

Some get noticed as they stay,
and disappear like a stone in water.

Some carry on un-noticed
And are missed in their absence.

Yet again, some are like flowers.
The petals drop down,
The beauty dies,
<u>But the fragrance stays!</u>

<u>9. To my li'l one, coming of age....</u>

Oh, my sweet li'l one,
isn't today special?
The day marking arrival
Of the woman that you are!

Know yourself, oh li'l one,
and preserve your identity.
Peep inward and you'll see
the changing fragrance of seasons within you,
and fresh shades and hues blending so naturally.

Looking at you,
I cannot but contain my outburst of happiness,
as an uneasy numbing fright crawls up my spine!

Turn...turn your ears sharply to me, my child!
These are artless words of fact unadorned,
Words as unsullied and pure
as milk oozing out of mother's bosom!

Breaking thread after thread
that kept you tethered,
as you wait impatiently
to unfurl your wings,
to glide up the sky
so invitingly vast and open,
dotted with hidden traps
that your guileless mind
and innocent eyes cannot spot,
I stand confused!

Am I seeing the me reflected in you?
Or is it a reflection of you within me?

But, dear one,
as you step into puberty,
as you get ready to take on
the mantle of womanhood,
are storms raging in your mind?

Do I see shadows of dark clouds in your eyes?
Does fear make you cringe?
oh, my honey, have a heart to recognise
the truth so horrid, to face the reality, so sour.

Forget not that we have amongst us,
a creed, known also as the male of the species.

Within homes or out,
do not ever, dear, dismiss the fact
that they are out there,
the vultures with frenzied minds,
the predators with a scowl on their faces.
Looking out for an opportunity
to maul you and shred you into pieces!

Listen, young one, to my words
filled but with pristine verity.
"Trust the males, do trust them like anyone else,
but never in surfeit and caution be your watchword.
Do not rest in that trust in a manner blind.
Never do gobble, but eat in small bites,
so you can keep chewing what you do bite off."

Honest, my cute, I do not have answers
for all your questions,
like how it is so and why it is so.
But to your question as to
which of the chunks among the creed
can be given your heedless trust,
let me tell you:
"On one segment of fellows, to be sure,
you can place blind trust, my lass,
and they are boys below ten years of age.
Then there is only one more chunk
that you can trust, and trust so implicitly.
Mark my words!
They are none other than
the males who have breathed their last."

Take care, my girl,
nurture a canny crow in your mind.
Wherever you venture out,
go free and bold,
but let the sharp crow-eyes guide you,
let the crow in you be quick enough
to step out of danger.

Oh, my lass, do not cower,
grow up, do grow in stature.
Do not cease from unleashing the power within you.
Give life to your dreams.
Be the life of earth, and
be the earth in spawning and sustaining life.

Oh my young one,
as you step out into womanhood,
my sweet wish to you is that like every true woman,
may you grow into that banyan tree
providing home and life to multitudes
<u>so silently, so ungrudgingly!</u>

<u>10. When loved ones depart...</u>

When loved ones depart,
They do not leave us quiet!

The silence they leave
Has a deafening echo.

The vacuum they create
Fills our space.

Time, they say, heals
All wounds.
Says who?

Take a look.
My time, the healer himself, is wounded.
And has been crawling along,
So agonisingly,
Ever since....,
<u>Like a snail!</u>

11. When you cry for no reason...

When you cry for no reason....,
Suddenly you realise,
You have lost something of value,
You don't know where.

When you cry for no reason.....,
Suddenly you realise,
you have travelled quite a distance,
But the horizon is still far away.

When you cry for no reason.....,
Suddenly you realise,
You, over time, have racked up quite a bit,
Yet it doesn't add up to anything.

When you cry for no reason.....,
suddenly you realise,
Love, as they say, is blind.
The loved one need not spot the person who loves.

When you cry for no reason......,
Suddenly you realise,
Time has stolen,
Without you ever noticing,
You from you!!!

<u>12. A true human.</u>

If you have a pair of eyes
that distinguishes light and colour,
yet incapable of seeing
pain and monstrosity around....,

If you have a pair of ears,
which can decipher sounds,
but not hear wails and cries
and moans surrounding you....,

If you have a tongue that can spit flames of fire,
yet not utter a word of cool comfort and empathy....,

If you have a pair of hands
which can reach out to touch and feel,
but not caress and soothe the fallen and way-laid....,

If you have a pair of legs
that moves you from place to place,
yet freezes on seeing hands raised
for help or support...,

If you have a body so stout
to defend you from harm,
which turns frail, when sought
as a prop for the feeble and infirm...,

If you have a mind that
can perceive everything under the sun,
yet cannot fathom
the plight of lives plundered and looted...,

Pat yourself.......Congratulate yourself!
You have become what you were wont to be;
You have become a true human being!

Everything in the heavens
and on earth is well put,
<u>And O human being, this is your kingdom!</u>

<u>13. Burning Embers.</u>

Reminiscences
are embers smouldering,
overlaid with ashes.
So innocently covered.

Barely any trace of heat or smoke
ever appear on the outside.

The inside tells a different story.
It's raging, red and searing hot.
Hanging fire!

A sudden gust charging from nowhere,
or a short stalk, or oil
or leaves falling on ash-top
and the embers leap their tongues out,
ready to consume you
<u>and your feeble world!</u>

<u>14. When we lose someone from our life...</u>

What happens when we lose
someone from our life?
Or, when someone decides
to kick it at your face and go?

Some move away in physical space,
even as the chemistry continues!

Some just choose to vanish
from every space around you!

Do we lose them from out of our life?
Or, do we lose a part of our life?

True, we haven't lost the book yet.
But where did we lose them, those pages in between?
The story, yet, advances ploddingly,
even with those paragraphs missing, pages torn off.

The book can, surely, be read!
But, somewhere, some connections go jumpy,
And life just moves painfully forward.
Tangled, a bit. Muddled, a bit!

The play moves on!
A few acts turn pallid!
The drama is missing.
<u>The melodrama continues!!!</u>

<u>15. When you laugh for no reason...</u>

When you laugh
And laugh for no reason,
You know you have made a lot of blunders in life,
And you are reliving them now!

When you laugh
And laugh for no reason,
You have reached the end of your sobbing,
And you are trying to force the last tear-drop out!

When you laugh
And laugh for no reason,
You are either a philosopher,
Or a lunatic,
And the difference is nothing major!

When you laugh
And laugh for no reason,
you have finally found the answer.
You arrive with a wail for no reason.
And the only true way out of life is
<u>A laugh for no reason!</u>

16. **Narcissus.**

I love the green lake.
Deep, weed-ridden,
Tranquil and serene.

Like a faded film,
A waning light spreads on the the secluded banks
On which small yellow pebbles lie scattered,
Round and shiny.

Here, are I sit lone on the shore,
Hugging my roots to my bosom,
In the fear I would lose them somewhere here.

Here, are I sit lone on the shore,
Throwing small yellow pebbles
At my concrete reflection
in the blue waters.

An abnormal euphoria envelopes me
when in the undulating rippling waters
my reflection dies away,
Deformed,
Convoluted,
Distorted.

With bitter resentment,
I turn away my eyes,
when I see them reunite
to give rebirth like a Jarasandha.

Suddenly creeps that strange sensation into my mind,
Making me aware of my entity.
With a wry smile I get up
To see darkness creeping into darkness
<u>Until you dissolve into that thick black fluid.</u>

17. The Black rock.

Indeed, the rock was black and ugly.
And it stood out,
From the grey ones.

Gross and sun-stroked
Was the Rock,
Like the girl
Who used to come to the sea shore,
Lonely.

The girl always cried,
When she looked at the rock,
Covering her face
With her slender arms.

Why does it un-quiet my heart
To see the girl crying?

Yesterday I dreamt that
I was transformed into the rock,
But grey!

I hate,
I hate the rock.

But, can you tell me,
Who painted the rock black?

<u>18. Blind games.</u>

Yes, love is blind.

But then, Blind is every game.
Every game starts with zero scores
And the finish is always a teaser!

Life and love are twin-twisters.
They are games
starting with "LOVE ALL" for everyone.

AND, it's bizarre at the end,
For The referee screams
at the top of his voice,
"l'oeuf"
Even at the finishing line.

Blind is love.
For, not all lovers know the truth.
There are no returns for their love.

Yes, Blindness is not a blot.
You cannot fault it.
Even your Eyes can,
many a time, deceive you.

Very often, your eyes only latch on to
the finishing line,
And you lose sight of
The race that you ran,
<u>The track and the people you ran with.</u>

<u>19. The game</u>

When the mundane turns a rarity,
expect the uncommon to transform to ordinary.

When your world goes for a toss,
You don't have a choice,
Heads you win, Tails you lose.
Maybe the batting. Maybe the bowling.
Playing the game is mandatory.

Winning or losing is not in our hands.
Play for the win, but be ready to lose.

What matters, when all is said and done, is but,
How elegantly you played, or,
How gracefully you carried the win
<u>or accepted the loss.</u>

20. Years ago.

Sun and seasons make their way.
You cannot ever leash them.
Let them go.

Years just go.
Let them.
You can never ever tether time.

They swish past.
They go their own way.
In a blink they just turn
"YEARS AGO"!
Let them go.

Do not make life static.
Let them go.
Those years!
Those years a-go!

Yes,
Years do make a go.

Not too long after,
You too have to make a go!!!

<u>21. My eGo!</u>

I want to say
Let Me Go.
Let mE GO

Go far from it.
Get away from it.
Just leave it.
Just leave it far away.

My mind won't.
It says: Let 'm go.
But, Let M-E-G-O!
Let m E G O!!!

And, It shouts,
How can u "let u go"?
Keep it.
Hold it.

Yes, let me hold my E G O!
<u>Isn't my ego, after all, dear to me?</u>